Giggle-Worthy

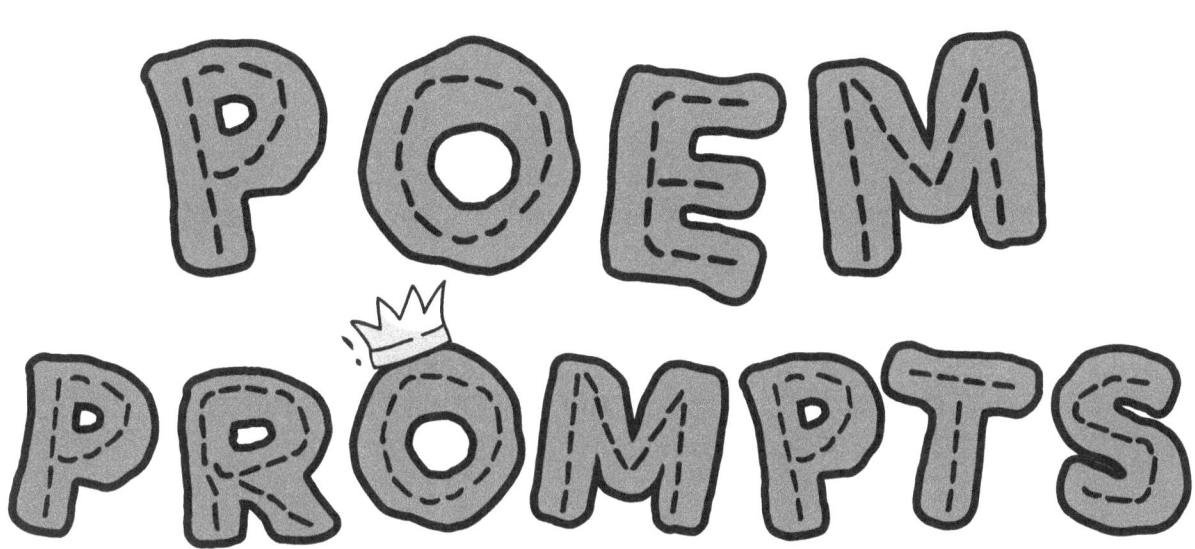

POEM PROMPTS

for kids

by Mike Downs
and Sandra K. Athans

RED WOLF
PRESS

Books for Young Writers from Red Wolf Press:

Poetry Prompts
Giggle-Worthy Poem Prompts for Kids by Mike Downs and Sandra Athans

Story Starters:
101 Story Starters for Little Kids by Maisy Day
101 Story Starters for Kids by Dena McMurdie
101 Story Starters for Teens by Maisy Day

Writing Prompts:
101 Writing Prompts for High School by Mark Trevor
101 Writing Prompts for Middle School by Mark Trevor
101 Writing Prompts for Grades 3-5 by Mark Trevor
101 Writing Prompts for Grades K-2 by Mark Trevor

Welcome to
Giggle-Worthy

POEM PROMPTS

for kids

A hilarious kid (and teacher) friendly bundle of fun!

Enjoy the **silliest, zaniest,** and most **fun-filled** poetry prompts with terrific top-tier tips for understanding and writing six types of poetry.

Kids will **giggle** and **laugh** as they learn simple techniques and tricks that will have them writing hilarious poems in record time!

Brought to you by:
Nationally renowned literacy expert and author Sandra K. Athans and quirky kid's poet and author Mike Downs.

RED WOLF
PRESS

To contact the publisher about permissions, send an email to dmcmurdie@redwolfpress.com.

ISBN: 978-1-955731-11-9

Published by Red Wolf Press.

Interior design and cover design by Dena McMurdie.

Cover art by depositphotos (mhatzapa) and Dena McMurdie.

First printing, March 2025.

Table of Contents

How to Use This Book

How to Use This Book:
Instructions for Kids

The most important rule is to have fun. Here's how you do it.

- Find the type of poetry you like the best.
- Find a poem prompt that tickles your funny bone.
- Figure out what you want to say.
- Then skedaddle and start writing!

TIP!

Some types of poems are more difficult to write than others. You may want to start with the simpler acrostic, free verse, or concrete poems. That's what we would do!

Remember, these are *your* poems. You can use the prompts, change them however you like, or make up your own. The sample poems we've supplied and the ideas in the prompts will help jiggle your brain and jumpstart your creative juices.

We'll also provide quick tips, helpful definitions, and fun facts. We want you to have fun! Fun! FUN!

Questions to ask yourself before you start writing:

- What is your poem about?
- Are there special patterns to follow? A set number of lines or syllables? Rules about rhymes?
- Do you want your poem to be funny, goofy, sweet, or sassy?
- Can you think of fun twists to add to your poem? Silly surprises? Oddball endings?

You'll find everything you need to answer these questions inside this book!

So... get ready... get set... GO!

...OOPS!

Wait a minute!

One more thing...

If any grownups are around, such as teachers, parents, caregivers, or others, take a peek at the next page.

How to Use This Book:
Instructions for Parents and Teachers

You can use this book in fun and flexible ways. Guide kids through the easy-to-grasp samples and prompts as main lessons in a poetry unit, or let them explore the workbook on their own. Here's a list of ideas:

Enrich classroom or homeschool lessons
- Use the examples, prompts, or tips to support your lesson plans on poetry.
- Use the book as a handy "go-to" poetry resource.

Morning work
- Assign poetry prompts from the book as special morning work.
- Add activities from the book into your daily morning routines.

Paired or group assignments
- Have kids write, read aloud, and critique in pairs or groups.
- Lead multiple small group instruction and review sessions.

Fun practice
- Use as extra activities for kids who finish classwork quickly.
- Offer during a rainy day recess, dismissal, or free time.

Support, extend, or add sparkle to basic skill-building
- Encourage kids to play with words and build vocabulary.
- Support kids' practice with rhyme patterns and breaking words into syllables.

Add-on extension activities
- Include prompts in journal writing activities.
- Add technology by composing prompts on a computer or iPad.

Extracurricular activities
- Launch an after-school poetry club.
- Perform an after-school poetry slam.

Let's try this again.

Ready. Set. GO. GO!

G OOOO O OO!!!

Amazing Acrostic Poems

What is an acrostic poem?

It's a poem in which the first letter of each line spells a word or phrase. The word or phrase can be whatever you want. Here's how to write one:

- Pick any word or short phrase.
- Write it vertically down the left side of a page. Use large capital letters. Here's an example using the name S-A-N-D-R-A (one of the authors of this book).
- Then, write words or phrases that begin with these capital letters. Write whatever you want. Sandra likes to keep things simple. She uses only one word per capital letter.

Sandra

Silly
Awesome
Nifty
Dramatic
Remarkable
Amazing

Notice that Sandra uses only a single word for each line. That's a great way to learn how to write acrostic poems! And yes, she is all of those wonderful things. When you write an acrostic poem with your name, you can use any words you like!

The other author, M-I-K-E, likes to make things more challenging. In this case, he wrote a whole poem about himself. Notice how he makes each line start wherever he wants so that the line begins with the correct letter.

Mike

Mike likes jellybeans
In his lettuce greens, with
Ketchup and salt, that he
Eats with a malt!

Mike's diet might be gross, but it does make a funny poem! And notice again how he starts each line wherever he wants. This puts the correct letter at the beginning of each line.

Acrostic poems are tons of fun and easy to make on your own. You can create one out of any word—including the word "word." Ha! So, let's go. You can write about pirates, dogs, pickles, or anything else you can imagine! As long as you can spell it.

Here are two more examples:

Fizzle

Fireworks
Ignite
Zooming
Zinging
Lickety-split
Exploding!

Dogs and Cats

Dogs yip and yap,
Or howl, and
Growl. Or
Sometimes, simply sleep.

And dozing dogs
Never nip at
Dear adorable cats.

Cats, however, purr and stir
And sometimes slyly slink
To tweak a
Sleeping dog. Oh my!

Now it's your turn! Use the prompts on the following pages to write your own amazing acrostic poems!

Me, Myself, & I Poem

Use the letters in your name to write an acrostic poem about you. Think of a great word that begins with each letter of your name to describe something special about you.

TIP!

Start by writing your name in capital letters in a line down the left side of the page. Start all your acrostic poems this way.

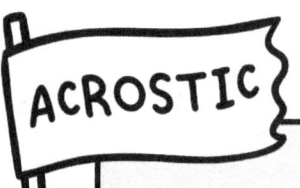

A Celebration Poem

What's your favorite holiday? Christmas? Kwanzaa? Valentine's Day? Groundhog Day? Write an acrostic poem that tells all about it. Picture how you celebrate the day in your mind like you're watching a movie. Then, think of words to describe what you see.

14

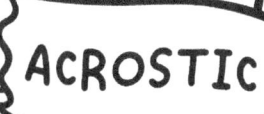

A Yummy Snack Poem

Is your favorite snack an ice cream sundae? Popcorn dripping in butter? A slab of beef jerky? Write a tasty acrostic poem about it. What words can you use to tell what it looks like, how it tastes, where you eat it, and why it's so yummy?

TIP!

Your acrostic poem can use one word or a few words to describe your chosen word.

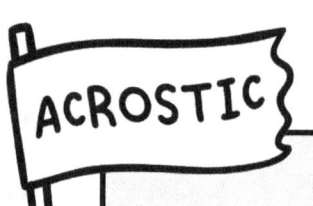

Special "Firsts" Poem

Special firsts are so much fun! Write an acrostic poem about your first day of school, the first day of summer break, your first splash in a giant mud puddle, or any other "first" that makes you jump for joy (even if it's not into a mud puddle)!

My Favorite Activity Poem

Write an acrostic poem about your favorite after-school activity. Do you play soccer? Dance? Attend a drama club or art club? What clever words can you think of that tell about your activity?

17

Gross Me Out Poem

Yuck! Ick! Barf! What food grosses you out? Brussels sprouts? Anchovies? Pickled pigs' feet? Write a funny acrostic poem about it. Tell what it looks like, how you react, or how you sneak it to your dog when no one's looking!

TIP!

Add words like "Yuck! Ick! Barf!" to make your poem funny and goofy. These are called **interjections (in-ter-JEK-shunzs)**. They're words that slip out of your mouth.

Superstar Poem

Write an acrostic poem using the name of a superstar you're bonkers over. It could be a superhero, celebrity, rockstar, or any other person you think is special. Use the letters in their name. Write about what they do, how they act, and what makes them so cool!

Pet Poem

Write an acrostic poem about any kind of pet. It can be your pet, a friend's pet, or a make-believe pet. You could make your acrostic poem using the word "dog," or you might use the dog's name, "Ruff." If you want a short poem, use short words like "cat" or "bird." If you want extra fun, try something like "alligator."

My Dream Getaway Poem

If you could be whooshed away to anywhere in the world, where would it be? A theme park, Yellowstone National Park, your Grandma's house, or Mount Everest? Name your special getaway and write an acrostic poem about it.

TIP!

Add a title to your acrostic poem. You can use the one from the prompt or make up your own!

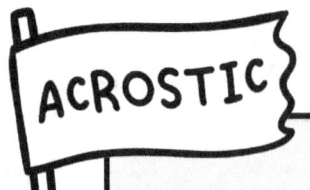

Amusement Ride Poem

Aaaah! Eek! Yikes! What ride gives you goosebumps and sends chills down your spine? Write an acrostic poem about a roller-coaster, Ferris wheel, Scrambler, or another ride that makes you SCREAM!

Fabulous Free Verse Poems

What is a free verse poem?

Let's start by saying what a free verse poem is not! A free verse poem does **not** have:

- special rules
- specific patterns
- required syllable counts
- rhyming requirements

Mostly, a free verse poem is a poem that has no rules—how cool is that?

Now, let's explain what a free verse poem is. A free verse poem is a poem where you write your words as they flow out of your brain. It can be any length. You can start or end sentences however you want. You can make your lines short or long. It's your choice. A free verse poem is like a free flow of your ideas to the page in a way that sounds good to *you!*

Turn the page to see a couple of examples of funny free verse poems.

Purple Pickles

Pickles.
Should not be purple.
Unless,
I guess.
Your eggplants are green.

This poem has one small rhyme in the middle (*unless, I guess*). It's okay to have a teeny, tiny bit of rhyme, but if it has too much, then it would not be a free verse poem.

The following example does not have any rhyme.

Tickles

I like tickles.
Feathers on my toes
Dancing fingers on my ribs
Gentle squeezes on my knees.

Giggling. Chortling.
Cackling. Howling.
Snorting! Roaring!

SHHHHH!!
Quiet in the classroom.

Now it's your turn! Use the prompts on the following pages to write your own fabulous free verse poems!

Winning a Competition

Write a free verse poem about winning a competition. It could be a dance competition, a race, or a ribbon your calf won at the local fair. You could describe how hard you worked, any jitters you had, how your award made you feel, or other ideas.

TIP!

Use super short or medium-sized sentences to make it look and sound awesome.

An Epic Blunder

Weird stuff happens! But an Epic Blunder... ugh! Write a poem about a time you faced an epic blunder. Did you fall off your chair at school? Maybe you laughed so hard that snot bubbles blew out of your nose. Write about what happened, describe how embarrassed you got, and how you recovered.

TIP!

Play with your words. Take a word like "laugh" and change it into "giggle," "chuckle," "titter," or "squeal."

A Nifty New Invention
of the Future

Put on your thinking cap and invent something extraordinary! Perhaps a new video game, a robot that does homework, or an automatic toilet opener and closer.

FREE VERSE

Your Million Dollar Mission

What would you do with ten million dollars? Buy a souped-up hot rod, a peppy pony, or a gazillion lollipops? Write a poem about your new super-rich life.

TIP!

The stranger or weirder your ideas are, the funnier your poem will be.

My Favorite Superhero: ME!

What superpower do you want? Write this poem about your new power. Can you disappear, fly, lift buildings, or stick out your tongue and catch tasty insects? How do you use this power?

The Purple Pickle Pancake Club

Write a poem about the most unusual food you can imagine putting in a pancake. Jellybeans? Spaghetti? Dog food? Purple pickles? What happens when someone eats it?

FREE VERSE

My New Store

Write a poem about a store you would like to open. Does your store sell bugs, frogs, lava rocks, balloons, kitty litter, or candy? What are your customers like? Do you charge them a lot of money or give things away?

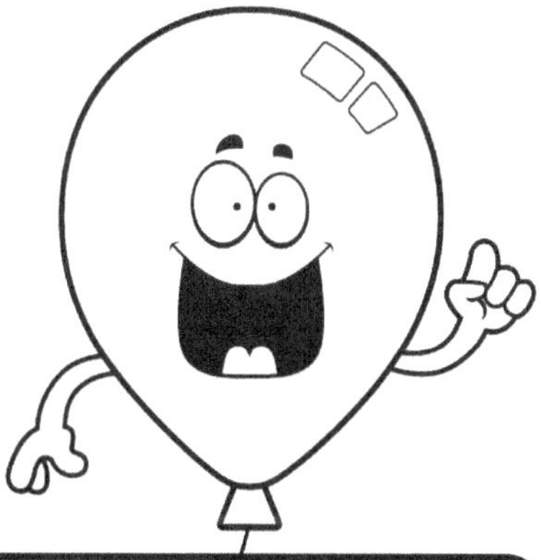

TIP!

Alliteration (uh-LIT-uh-RAY-shun) is fun! Words that start with the same letter make your poems sound even better. Try three words in a row, like "big bad balloons" or "fluffy flying frogs."

What a Club!

Write a poem about a make-believe club you plan on joining. It could be a club that raises alien beetles, collects rolls of toilet paper, stacks chairs on top of bowling balls, or paints cucumbers. What is a club meeting like?

My Favorite Hobby

Write a poem about a hobby you like. It could be playing video games, riding bikes, or reading books. Or write a silly poem about a hobby you don't want to do. Maybe something like collecting poison ivy or tasting hot sauces.

TIP!

If you find it hard to start, describe your topic in the first few lines. If you write a poem about hot sauce, it might start like this:

The hot sauce was spicy, and smelly, and gloopy and gloppy.

Spooky Adventure

Write a poem about a spooky adventure. It could be going into a haunted house, walking through a bug-filled room, or chasing ghosts through a cemetery.

Incredible Concrete Poems

What is a concrete poem?

A concrete poem is written in the shape of whatever the poem is about. If you write about an airplane, you'd write your poem in the shape of a plane. If you write about a mountain, you'd write your poem in the shape of a mountain. You can even play with letters and make them BIG or small.

The easiest way to write a concrete poem is to start with a simple drawing of the subject you want to write about. Then, write your poem alongside or inside the drawing. If you practice enough, you might even be able to write a poem in a special shape without using a drawing to help you. Either way, have fun!

A concrete poem can rhyme if you want it to—or be free verse or any other kind of poem. The only rule is that the poem must have some type of shape.

Turn the page to see a few examples of concrete poems.

The Mighty Oak Tree

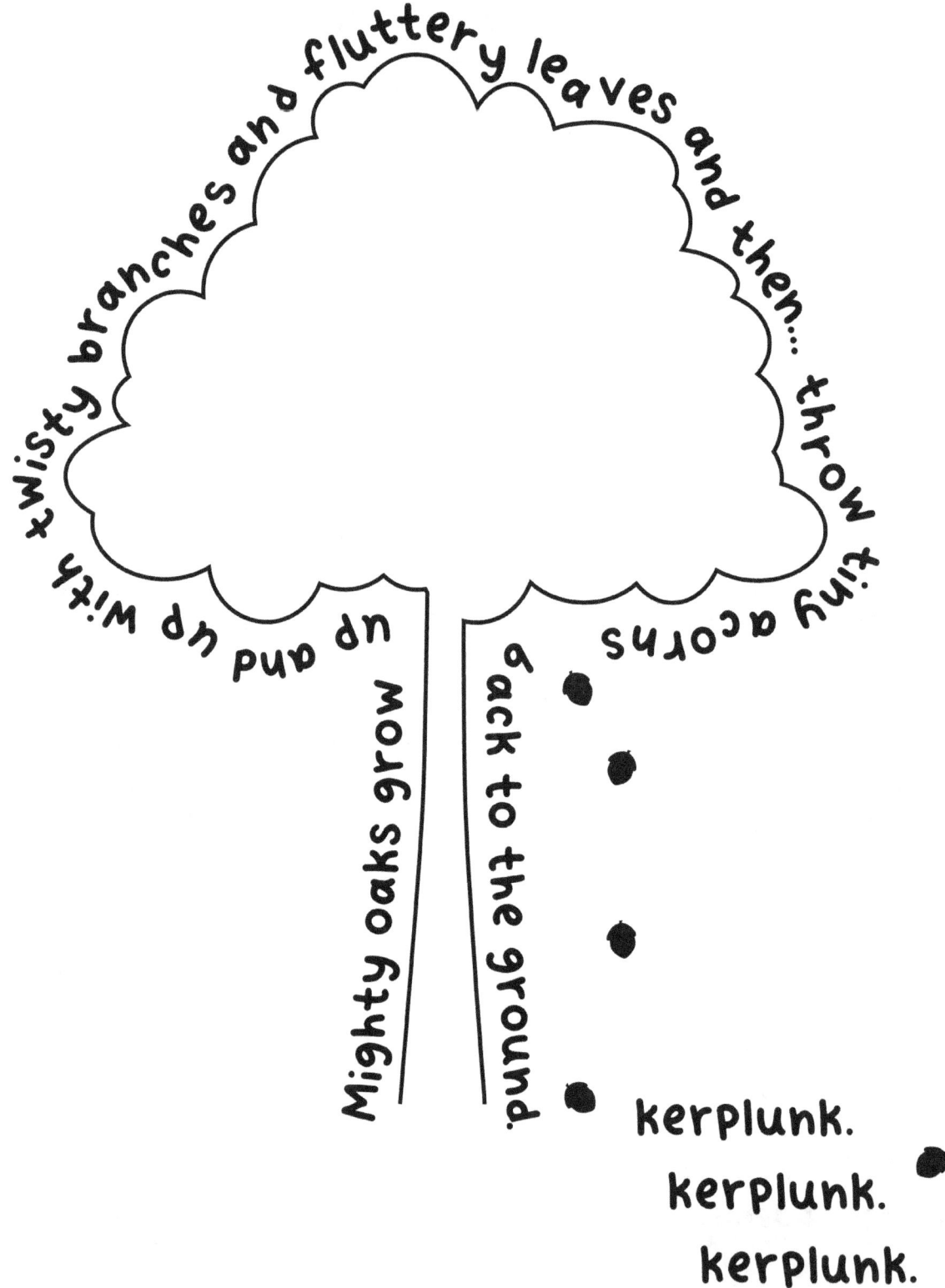

Mighty oaks grow up and up with twisty branches and fluttery leaves and then... throw tiny acorns back to the ground. kerplunk. kerplunk. kerplunk.

36

BIG CIRCLE. small circle.

The Simple Square

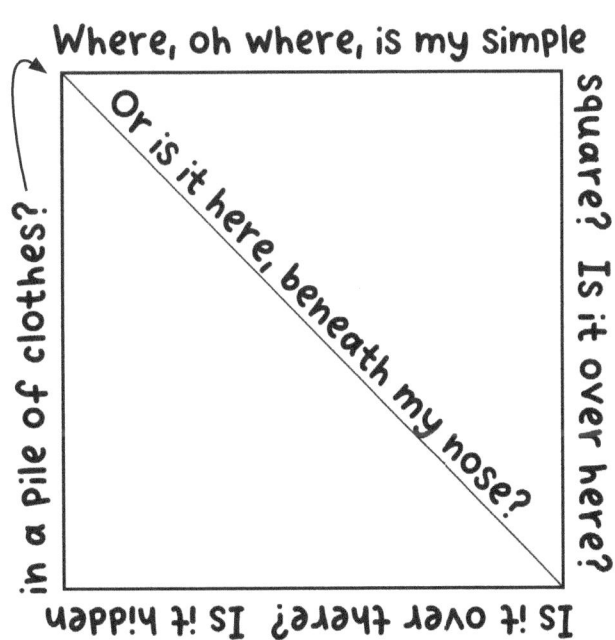

Now it's your turn! Use the prompts on the following pages to write your own incredible concrete poems!

CONCRETE POEMS

Helping Hand Poem

Draw your hand lightly (use a separate piece of paper if needed). On the traced line, write a poem describing a few ways you like to "lend a hand" and help others. How do you help your teacher? Your parents? A neighbor? Your friends? Share your helpful ways in your poem.

TIP!

Here's a super trick! Draw your shape very lightly with a regular pencil. Then, write the poem on your shape, using colored pencils, gel pens, or thin-tipped markers. Next, wait a few minutes for the ink to dry, then erase the regular pencil. VOILA! You have a super-duper concrete poem with no lines showing!

I Stepped in It! Poem

To "step in it" means you've done something by mistake—with red-faced embarrassment or BIG trouble as a result. Draw a foot or shoe. Write a funny poem about a time you stepped in it! Did you blurt out news about a surprise birthday party? Did you give your grandma dog treats, thinking they were human snacks? Or did you step on something like dog poop? Yikes!

Crazy Animal Poem

Draw the weirdest animal you can think of. It might have 13 arms and legs or be a gloppy blob. Write a funny poem about how it looks, what it eats, or how it travels, swims, or flies around the world.

Geometric Shape Poem

Draw your favorite shape—maybe a circle, square, triangle, or squircle (a cross between a square and a circle)! Ha! Write your poems about objects that look like the shape. For example, a circle can be used to write a poem about the moon or an orange. A triangle is perfect to write about an Egyptian pyramid or a shark tooth. Let your imagination go wild!

TIP!

Look around you for objects with familiar or unfamiliar shapes. Use one of them!

Scribble Poem

Instead of using shapes in your concrete poem, use a doodle, a scribble, a swirl, or a starburst. These fanciful designs can add whimsy and sparkle to your poem. Write about a fireworks display, tossed confetti, or yummy sprinkles on a giant sugar cookie!

Lopsided Letter Poem

Concrete poems can also use fancy letters that look like the fun fonts you use on a computer or iPad. Mix capital letters with lowercase letters. Use fat and skinny letters. Try out giant-sized letters jumbled up with teeny-tiny letters! Add polka dots to your letters! The fun never stops!

TIP!

Try writing the letters of your name in silly, crazy shapes, and imagine the goofy things you can write around those letters.

Oddball Lines Poem

Concrete poems can also be written on weird lines. Write about a runaway balloon on a line that stretches skyward. Write about some ups and downs on a line that looks like a staircase. Write about a dinner disaster on lines resembling a spilled box of uncooked spaghetti noodles.

Upside-Down Poem

This one is great! Turn your workbook upside down and draw whatever you want. Then, write a poem about why everything is upside down. Is it because of an earthquake? The wind? An alien monster? When you're done, turn the book right-side up.

Artistic Poem

If you're a budding artist, draw the shape of your favorite animal, a special person, or an interesting object you see outside your window. Then, write about it on the outline, inside it, or both. The sky's the limit!

TIP!

If your shape doesn't look good, write a poem about why the shape looks so silly.

Stick Figure Poem

If you can't draw, don't worry. Use stick figures! Draw a barnyard with stick figure animals. Label the figures—horses, chickens, barn cats, etc., and write poems about the animals on the lines of their stick bodies. Use this fun idea for other scenes, too.

What is an epitaph poem?

First, let's talk about what a simple epitaph is. An epitaph is a short, written statement about someone who died. You usually find epitaphs on gravestones. An example might be:

A wonderful friend who made the world a better place.

Or:

Gone but not forgotten.

Or:

To a colorful person who loved rainbows.

But in our workbook, we'll write **goofy, silly,** or **giggly** epitaphs.

Write these in any style that you like. They can rhyme or not—whatever you want!

Here are a few examples of funny epitaph poems.

The Banana Eater

Here lies a lazy man who loved bananas
but threw the peels on the floor.
Until he slipped on one.

The Fisherman

Here's a man who liked to fish
and make a tasty seafood dish.
Until he took an ocean swim
and met a shark that gobbled him!

The Texter

Here lies a man who liked to text
while driving down the street.
It's obvious what happened next—
he lies beneath my feet.

> Now it's your turn! Use the prompts on the following pages to write your own hilarious epitaph poems!

Epitaph
Poems

How Did That Happen?

Write an epitaph about someone (a make-believe person) who died in a silly way. Maybe by:

- Giggling too much
- Sleepwalking off a cliff
- Swallowing a fly

TIP!

Try drawing a special gravestone, then write your epitaph poem on it.

A Bug's End

Write an epitaph about a blood-sucking pest that bit some-one, and then the *bug* died. Here are a few blood-smacking critters:

- Tick
- Flea
- Leech

Life Cycle Epitaph

Write an epitaph about a creature's lifecycle stages. Use all of the stages or any you choose:

- Butterfly (egg, larva, chrysalis, adult)
  Example: *The caterpillar had to die but then became a butterfly!*
- Frog (egg, tadpole, froglet, adult frog)
- Dandelion (seed, germination, rosette, flowering, seed head)

TIP!

It's fun to use your rhyming skills in these poems. You can start by thinking of words that rhyme with the words in the prompt.

Once Upon an Ending

Write an epitaph about a well-known fairy tale character. Here are a few to get you started.

- Humpty Dumpty
- The wolf from *The Three Little Pigs*
- The witch from *Hansel and Gretel*

Epitaph Poems

Doomed Daredevils

Write an epitaph about an unusual sports daredevil. Have fun imagining how each of these athletes met their death:

- Ping-Pong player
- Hula-Hoop hipster
- Video gamer

Alive Again

Write an epitaph about a creature that does not die. Get creative with the oddballs on this list:

- A cat with nine lives
- A zombie
- A ghost

TIP!

Like many poems, these are super fun to read aloud. To add to the silliness of your epitaph, read it aloud with a sad, somber face. The mismatched mix is hysterical!

Epitaph Poems

Remember When...

Write an epitaph about something you've outgrown. We've all felt a tragic loss over these:

- A baby blanky
- Your best-loved sneakers
- A bad habit—nose picking, jumping in mud puddles, burping LOUDLY in class

A Fast Finish

Write a speedy epitaph about a slow animal. We've listed a few rhyming words to help you get started.

- Snail (sail, pail, tail)
- Sloth (cloth)
- Slug (bug, rug, mug)

TIP!

Use a rhyming dictionary to help you find rhyming words. Once you have words that rhyme, you can make a silly poem with them.

How Long Has That Been There?

Write an epitaph about stinky, gross, or "left-for-dead" food.

- Squishy black bananas
- Moldy sandwiches
- Crusty scrambled eggs

The Good Old Days

Write an epitaph about something old-fashioned or no longer around.

- Old video game
- Favorite fast-food treat
- Cursive writing (who even knows what that is anymore?)

59

cool Haiku

Poems

What is a haiku?

A haiku is a poem that has a very special pattern. In this case, it has a strict syllable pattern. Here's how it works:

A haiku has three lines.
- The first line has five syllables.
- The second line has seven syllables.
- The third line has five syllables.

> A syllable is one unit of sound that is pronounced in a word. The word "hi" has one syllable. The word "hello" has two syllables. The sentence "I have a pink dog" has five syllables.

For most haikus:
- Line one sets the scene.
- Line two adds more information.
- Line three is a surprise, a twist, something you notice, or something that happens because of the first two lines.

Haikus are mostly written about nature, noticing simple things, or seeing the world around us. Here is a haiku about what someone might see and think as they watch ocean waves.

Waves

Waves churn into foam,
Roaring lines of frothy white,
Vanish in silence.

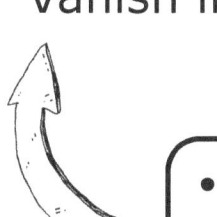

- Notice how the first line sets the scene for the poem. It's about foamy waves.
- The second line adds new details about the waves. We have long lines of roaring waves now.
- The third line adds a conclusion or closing thought that's easy to "see" in your mind. It says that the roaring waves vanish into silence.

But wait! You don't have to write about nature. You can also write a silly or goofy haiku. Have fun when you write your own!

Turn the page to see a couple of examples of cool haiku poems.

Dirty Laundry

Mud puddles beckon,
Children leap and splash and splat,
Mountains of laundry.

1. Notice how the first line sets the scene for the poem. It's about mud puddles.

2. The second line adds new information related to the mud puddles. We discover that kids are jumping and splashing in them.

3. The third line has a funny twist—the muddy leaping and splashing results in piles of dirty laundry.

The Dentist

Lying back, eyes wide,
Mouth agape. Noisy drilling.
Happy teeth again.

In this haiku, we learn about a trip to the dentist's office. What will your haiku be about?

Use your senses and feelings as you think about ideas for your haiku. This will help you set the scene of your poem, add details, and create pictures using words.

- What do you see?
- What action words describe the scene?
- What do you hear?
- What do you taste?
- What do you smell?
- What might it feel like?
- What emotions do you have?
- What can you compare it to?

Your haiku might use a few or all of these ideas. In the following prompts, pick and choose words from the lists we've supplied, or use your own words.

Now it's your turn! Use the prompts on the following pages to write your own cool haiku poems!

Looking Up

Write a haiku about clouds or something in the sky. Your ideas could include:

- See: fluffy, feathery, white, gray-blue, dark clouds (you might also see rain, snow, sleet)
- Action words: skim, float, race, prance
- Hear: distant rumbling, far-away claps of thunder
- Touch: cool, sticky, moist, damp
- Makes me feel: creative, joyful, scared
- Comparisons: cotton, comfy quilt, puffy pillow, cloaks

TIP!

Haikus are often written about nature. Go outside and look around. Breathe in. Breathe out. Take it all in! Something will spark your interest (maybe even a buzzing bee chasing the janitor.)

Little Critters

Write a haiku about a snake, lizard, or frog. Your ideas could include:

- See: slender, compact, chubby, black, green-gray
- Action words: slither, scoot, hop, wallow
- Hear: hiss, snarl, croak, rustling leaves, plops of water
- Smell: swampy, musky, fishy
- Touch: smooth, pimply, slick
- Makes me feel: squirmy, excited, horrified
- Comparisons: garden hose, sneaky beast

TIP!

An easy way to know how many syllables are in a word is to clap the units of sound in the word. "Hi," takes one clap. "Hello," takes two claps.

Let's Celebrate!

Write a haiku about a birthday party or other celebration. Your ideas could include:

- See: balloons, presents, games, friends, crowds
- Action words: rollick, frolic, whirl, twirl
- Hear: giggles, squeals, singing, buzzing
- Taste: chocolate cake, strawberry ice cream, lemonade
- Makes me feel: like a superstar, wired up, special
- Comparisons: ceremony, star-studded gala, national holiday

TIP!

Use comparisons to give your poetry more expressive feelings. For example, "A comfy hug is like a warm blanket around me." When two different things are compared using the words "like" or "as," the technique is called a **simile (SIM-uh-lee)**.

Show Me the Money

Write a haiku about money or an allowance. Your ideas could include:

- See: shiny discs, copper, silver, presidents, rumpled paper, rectangles, green
- Action words: spill, wobble, spin, stack
- Hear: jingling, clinking, rumpling, scrunching
- Touch: hard, cool, worn, crisp
- Makes me feel: rich, like a millionaire, lucky
- Comparisons: gold, treasure, loot

TIP!

Another way to compare things is with a **metaphor (MET-uh-for)**. A metaphor does not use the words "like" or "as" when making a comparison. It simply puts the comparison words together. An example would be "a mountain of money."

Haiku

Long Gone

Write a haiku about a lost item or something that broke. Your ideas could include:

- See: heaps of tossed clothes, disheveled drawers, shattered pieces, busted parts
- Action words: dashing, scurrying, splintering, collapsing
- Hear: moans, groans, crashes, bangs
- Makes me feel: mad, rushed, bumbling, doomed
- Comparisons: treasure hunt, spinning in circles, bull in a china shop, clumsy oaf

Game-tastic!

Write a haiku about a video game. Your ideas could include:

- See: friends sprawled on the floor, lit up iPads, flicking fingers, squirmy bodies
- Action words: herky-jerky, pounding, flailing, wiggly
- Hear: gasps, groans, cheers, guffaws
- Touch: buttons, plastic goggles, sweaty palms
- Makes me feel: thrills, jumpy, ecstatic, pounding heart
- Comparisons: command center, jungle of wild beasts, winning team's locker room

TIP!

Remember that a haiku has only three lines.

- Line one is five syllables.
- Line two is seven syllables.
- Line three is five syllables.

Pee-yew!

Write a haiku about stinky sneakers or smelly clothes. Your ideas could include:

- See: busted shoelaces, grimy stains, sticky goop, crusty flakes
- Action words: tossed, worn out, ruffled, twisted
- Smell: dirty feet, mold, sweat
- Touch: slimy, gritty, gooey, worn
- Makes me feel: gasping for air, near death, fighting to survive
- Comparisons: heaping laundry bin, crowded locker room, like wearing a sweaty sock

....
....
....
....
....
....
....
....

TIP!

Add words like "Argh! Boink! Awww! YUCK!" to bring extra action and feeling into your poem. This is called **Onomatopoeia (AH-no-MAH-tuh-PEE-uh)**. These are words that are spelled the way they sound.

At the Fair

Write a haiku about a county fair. Your ideas could include:

- See: animal exhibits, contests, silly games, craft booths
- Action words: showing off, chomping, sweating
- Hear: music, cheering, clucking, chortling
- Taste: corn dogs, pies, lemonade
- Smell: caramel apples, manure, pumpkin pies, hay
- Makes me feel: excited, happy, surprised, amazed
- Comparisons: Old-fashioned fun, fanciful critters, eye-popping competitions

Haiku

Note-Worthy

Write a haiku about a musical instrument. Your ideas could include:

- See: guitar, piano, cello, drums, violin bow
- Action words: buzzing, vibrating, pounding
- Hear: pounding, screeching, twanging, plunking
- Smell: musty theater, lemon wax, rosin
- Touch: plucking strings, banging keys, skimming bow
- Makes me feel: happy, sad, excited, sleepy
- Comparisons: roaring crowd, stirring breeze

TIP!

The longest English word is **pneumonoul-tramicroscopicsilicovolcanoconiosis**, with 19 syllables. Don't try using this word in a haiku because it has more syllables than an entire haiku poem!

Furry Friends

Write a haiku about a favorite animal. Your ideas could include:

- See: dog, cat, bear, sloth, anteater, lion
- Action words: pounce, belly crawl, stalk, meander
- Hear: roaring, hissing, yapping, yowling
- Smell: stinky litter, wet fur, smelly poop, freshly washed
- Touch: fuzzy, soft, wiry, prickly
- Makes me feel: cozy, scared, playful, curious
- Comparisons: slow as a snail, speedy as a jet

Super Lit

Limericks

What is a limerick?

A limerick is a poem that rhymes in a special pattern. Here's how it works:

A limerick has five lines.
- The 1st, 2nd, and 5th lines must rhyme with each other. These lines have 7-10 syllables.
- The 3rd and 4th lines rhyme, but it must be a different rhyme. These lines have 5-7 syllables.

> Limericks are especially fun because most of them are written to be silly, funny, or goofy.

For most limericks:
- The first two lines start a story.
- The next two lines bring something new into the story.
- The final line adds a silly twist.

Here are two examples of limericks:

A Cucumber Named Fred

A handsome cucumber named Fred,
was admired in a vegetable bed.
But a vinegar bath
set him straight on the path
to becoming a pickle instead.

- The first two lines rhyme and introduce the story. It's about a handsome cucumber named Fred.
- The next two lines rhyme separately. They tell us something new about Fred, the handsome cucumber. We learn he is taking a bath in vinegar.
- The final line must rhyme with lines one and two. It also adds a silly twist: We learn that the vinegar bath has turned Fred into a pickle.

Sneaky Ted

1. There once was a youngster named Ted (8 syllables)
2. Whose room was a mess, so he said, (8 syllables)
3. "I know what to do, (5 syllables)
4. I'll hide stuff from view (5 syllables)
5. And sweep it all under my bed." (8 syllables)

- Notice how lines one, two, and five rhyme.
- Lines three and four also rhyme.

Now it's your turn! Use the prompts on the following pages to write your own super lit limericks!

Dirty Jobs

Write a limerick about a yucky chore you don't want to do.

- Taking out trash
- Making your bed
- Cleaning up pet poop

Why Though?

Write a limerick about a silly school rule.

- No running in hallways
- No pets in school
- No food fights in the cafeteria

TIP!

How to make a laugh-out-loud limerick:

1. Give your character a silly habit that gets them into trouble.
2. Have your character face a sticky challenge that they solve in an odd way.
3. Make your character want something ridiculous, resulting in a goofy outcome.
4. Put your character in a nutty situation that they handle cleverly.

Imaginary Bestie

Write a limerick about a pretend friend.

- An odd animal (orangutan, platypus, skunk)
- An invisible creature (alien, monster, your shadow)
- An electronic oddball (a whacky robot, pesky drone, video game villain)

TIP!

Limericks are meant to be read aloud! So... CRANK UP THE VOLUME! Share them aloud with friends, parents, teachers, and the pile of stuffed animals snoozing on your bed!

Oddball Insects

Write a limerick about a weird bug. Does it drive cars? Play video games?

- Cockroach
- Fruit fly
- Larva (almost a bug)

TIP!

Even if your character isn't a person, you can make it act like one! **Personification (per-son-uh-fuh-KAY-shun)** is when you give "person" traits to a "nonperson." Your cockroach could be a champion gamer! Your fruit fly might sing the blues! You can make your larva a famous brain surgeon!

Anything Can Be a Pet

Write a limerick about an unusual pet.

- Gorilla
- T-Rex
- Banana (that's super unusual!)

TIP!

Silly surprises can add hysterics to your limerick! A banana for a pet? C'mon!

Veggie Misfits

Write a limerick about a strange-looking vegetable. Does it go to a beauty contest and win? Does it scare the other vegetables?

- Radish
- Lima bean
- Ginger root

Thrills and Chills

Write a limerick about a creepy monster. Does it chase people? Hide under the bed? Make chocolate pudding?

- Swamp beast
- Bigfoot
- Bogeyman

TIP!

Following patterns is hard... at first! But like any skill, the more you practice, the better you get. Soon, you'll become a pro!

That's Unexpected

Write a limerick about an awkward animal. Does it tell jokes? Eat at a dining room table?

- Sloth
- Slug
- Anteater

TIP!

Say the *opposite* for fun! For example, ants are always busy and known as hard workers. So, in your limerick, you might call an ant "lazy." Or, you might mention a "speedy" sloth. It makes no sense, right? This is the opposite of what we usually think. Our brains picture these animals differently, which makes this idea funny!

Do Not Eat!

Write a limerick about a stinky refrigerator leftover.

- Fish
- Cheese
- Egg salad

Rock 'n' Roll

Write a limerick about a rock with a name. Maybe it likes to dance, skip across the water, or show off.

- Lava
- Diamond
- Pebble

Techniques for Writing
Amazing Poems

Here's a quick review of some writing techniques we've introduced throughout the book.

Alliteration (uh-LIT-uh-RAY-shun)

Use words that start with the same letter to make your poems especially excellent! Excitement explodes when your poem includes awesome alliteration.

Comparisons

Come up with comparisons that make things more fun.

- **Metaphors (MET-uh-forz)** compare things without the words "like" or "as." For example, *a mountain of mashed potatoes* (describing a lot of mashed potatoes) or *a sea of meowing furballs* (describing a lot of cats).
- **Similes (SIM-uh-leez)** compare things using the words "like" or "as." For example, *a pig as big as a hippo* or *a bug like a squished raisin with legs.*

Interjections (in-ter-JEK-shunzs)

These are short, expressive words that pack a lot of emotion. They are often sounds that show surprise, shock, or joy. Some examples include *wow, uh-oh, ouch, hooray, ick, yuck,* and *psst.*

Onomatopoeia (AH-no-MAH-tuh-PEE-uh)

These words are spelled the way they sound. Use plenty of these for extra fun. Here are a few examples: *bang, crash, hiss, sizzle, gurgle, creak, meow, boing,* and *woof.*

Opposites

For added fun, describe things as the opposite of what they are or in confusing ways. Talk about a *speedy snail*, a *teensy grizzly bear*, a *jumbo dwarf*, or a *muddy bath*.

Personification (per-son-uh-fuh-KAY-shun)

This is when you give "person" traits to a "nonperson." You can make leaves *dance* in the breeze. Have your squeaky bike *complain* as you pedal it. Have the sun *peek* over the horizon.

Playful Words

Take boring words and make them exciting. Instead of *walking*, you might *trot, skip,* or *hike.* Instead of *flying*, an airplane might *zoom, zip,* or *roar* through the sky.

Rhyming Dictionary

A rhyming dictionary will introduce lots of great new rhyming words to help unleash your inner poet.

About the Authors

SANDRA K. ATHANS

Sandra K. Athans is a published literacy specialist and a former classroom teacher. She is also an award-winning children's author. Her children's books are a mix of playfulness, adventure, and fun! More at sandraathans.com.

MIKE DOWNS

Mike is the author of more than 35 books for children. He's written geography, aerospace, fantasy, memoir, and poetry. Mike is also a USAF Academy graduate with a master's degree in aviation science. More at mikedownsbooks.com.

IMAGE CREDITS:

Front cover: background: Dena McMurdie, all images depositphotos—fox, flower, crown, lightbulb, shooting star, dinosaur, man with umbrella, hearts, ladybug, doodles: mhatzapa, folded paper: jannystockphoto.

Back cover: background: Dena McMurdie, all images depositphotos—frog, crown, leaf, raincloud, butterflies, planet, sock, leaves, hot air balloon, pencil, pineapple, x doodles, cat, fish skeleton, tree, apple, arrow, rabbit: mhatzapa; paper with clip: jannystockphoto.

Interior: Pages 1-35, all images depositphotos. **Page 1-3:** folded paper: jannystockphoto, **2:** dog: Natuska, **3:** doodle: mhatzapa, **4:** retro flying saucer: lhfgraphics, **5-6:** rhinoserous, panda: cthoman, **7:** chicken with stop sign: ronleishman, **8-10:** lizard teacher, pencil, dog and banner: cthoman; superhero: marish; marker lines: Bakai **11:** jelly bean, malt: nkiseleva1.gmail.com; lettuce: izakowski; ketchup, salt: larryrains; fireworks: tartila.stock.gmail.com; marker lines: Bakai **12:** sleeping dog, pouncing cat, sofa: ronleishman; marker line: Bakai, **13:** rabbit knight: cthoman; flag: stolenpencil, **14:** gifts, balloons, starbursts, ribbon, doodles: tartila.stock.gmail.com, **15:** frog: cthoman, **16:** boy jumping in puddle: IvanNikulin, **17:** boy painting: Katerina_Dav, **18:** food: ronleishman; dragon: cthoman, **19:** superhero rabbit: marish, **20:** cat and dog: AlonaS1984, **21:** airplane: godfather744431; cat: cthoman, **22:** roller coaster ride: ronleishman, **23:** pencil holding sign, arrow: cthoman, **24:** pickle, eggplant: cthoman; laughing child, shushing teacher: ronleishman; marker lines: Bakai; arrow: orfeev, **25:** banner: stolenpencil; award ribbon: lhfgraphics, star: cthoman, **26:** bird: cthoman, **27:** robot: SketchMaster, **28:** rabbit: cthoman, **29:** superhero raccoon: marish, **30:** dog chef: ronleishman, **31:** balloon: cthoman, **32:** boy scout troop: ronleishman, **33:** chili pepper: cthoman, **34:** ghost: ronleishman, **35:** dinosaur, arrow: cthoman.

36-37: tree with acorns, circles, box: Dena McMurdie; marker lines: Bakai (depositphotos).

Pages 38-89 all images depositphotos. **Page 38-43:** fish, pig, leopard: cthoman, **46:** paintbrush: MisterElements, **48:** red panda: cthoman, **49:** banana peel: larryrains; shark: nataliahubbert; boy texting: ronleishman; marker lines: Bakai, **50-52:** gravestone: HitToon, porcupine, tick, butterfly: cthoman, **53-55:** wolf, hula hooping bear, cat: ronleishman, **56:** shoes: stolenpencil, **57:** snail: cthoman, **58-59:** picky eater, boy playing video game: ronleishman, **60:** cow with banner: cthoman, **61:** waves: Seamartini; marker lines: Bakai; star, smiling arrow: cthoman; arrow: orfeev, **62:** muddy boy: ronleishman; marker lines: Bakai; happy tooth: Indie-Design; arrow: orfeev, **63:** lion: cthoman, bear with pencil: ronleishman, **64-66:** banner: Quilli; cloud, lizard, cake: cthoman **67-68:** rich pig, bear with broken kite: ronleishman, **69:** octopus: cthoman, **70-71:** boy with stinky sock, boy playing fair game: ronleishman, **72:** girl with guitar: Katerina_Dav, **73:** moose: cthoman, **74:** ladybug, arrow: cthoman, **75:** cucumber: Mictoon; marker lines: Bakai; arrow: orfeev, **76:** wooden sign: Quilli; boy raking leaves: ronleishman, **77:** sheep: cthoman, **78:** girl with monster: Katerina_Dav, **79-80:** insect, ram: cthoman, **81:** onion spraying deodorant: ronleishman, **82-83:** cyclops, penguin: cthoman, **84:** cat holding fish bones: ronleishman, **85:** happy rock: cthoman, **86:** shooting star: cthoman, **87:** boy with big backpack, girl with big backpack, dog with backpack: ronleishman, **88:** frames: mhatzapa, author photos provided by the authors, **89:** dog reading: cthoman.

www.ingramcontent.com/pod-product-compliance
Lightning Source LLC
Chambersburg PA
CBHW080127150626

46550CB00017B/2781